On the Way:
Lenten Reflections On Our Journey to Easter

On the Way

Unless otherwise indicated, scripture quotations are from The ESV® Bible (The Holy Bible, English Standard Version®), copyright © 2001 by Crossway, a publishing ministry of Good News Publishers. Used by permission. All rights reserved.

ISBN 978-0-9895633-6-9 (print)
ISBN 978-0-9895633-7-6 (eBook)

Welcome to

On the Way:

Lenten Reflections On Our Journey to Easter.

Whether you have chosen this devotional as an alternative to your usual practice during this season or are new to Lent altogether and seeking some focus, it is my hope and prayer that it will provide you with some needed space to become more fully abandoned to God.

The purpose of Lent devotions is usually two-fold. First, it gives us all time to prepare our hearts, to weed out anything that has been hiding in the corners of our hearts. It gives us space to inhale God's truths, and exhale some of our own 'stuff' that we've been holding onto.

A Lent devotional also shines some perspective on the events in the life of Jesus that reflect onto the Resurrection. His words, his actions, his prayers. All of his life was focused on that day, so we can learn something from his whole life that will brighten our Easter even more.

On the Way

This Lent devotional does a little of both. But it also may take you in directions that are even deeper. Enjoy your journey wherever it takes you.

Starting on Ash Wednesday through the day before Easter, this devotional covers six weeks – a total of 40 daily devotions that include Scripture readings, and some thoughts on them. NOTE: It does not have an entry for any of the Sundays, a day of rest even from this devotional (;o)

My prayer is that it brings you peace and perspective in this wonderful season of celebration!

~Diane

The good shepherd lies down

his life for the sheep.

~John 10.11

On the Way

Are You Ready?

READINGS: PSALM 51; MATTHEW 6.16-18

This is a new beginning. Or it may be just a continuation of your normal.

As we embark on this Lenten journey, let us seriously consider what we are committing to doing.

Is it to sit in obedience to God's word, or is it to put on a good show; maybe even the same show we've been putting on for decades? Fasting on something worldly. Praying at the "appropriate" times for all to see. Opening up the Bible 40 times without *hearing* anything.

> *Do you think all God wants are sacrifices – empty rituals just for show? He wants you to listen to him! Plain listening is the thing, not staging a lavish religious production. ~1 Samuel 15.22 {MSG}*

As we enter into this Lenten season, let's not enter into it lightly.

Rather, let's commit to taking this seriously, putting effort into listening to God. And in the back of our minds to constantly be engaging our hearts with this whisper - Am I Listening to God?

Have You Turned Away?

READINGS: LUKE 24.46-48

The ritual involving ashes emerged from the purity laws in the days of Moses. A red heifer cow was sacrificed by fire, then the ashes from that fire purified the 'water for impurity.' This *special* water was then used to purify anyone who touched a dead corpse. (Numbers 19)

Just like the ashes of a red cow, the ashes you may have received yesterday, have no magic powers. But just as they represented a purifying in the days of Moses, they represent a need for purifying our hearts today.

For if the blood of goats and bulls,
and the sprinkling of defiled persons
with the ashes of a heifer, sanctify
them for the purification of the flesh,
how much more will the blood of
Christ, who through the eternal Spirit
offered himself without blemish to
*God, **purify our consciences** from*
dead works to serve the living God.
~Hebrews 9.13-14

The act of purification, with or without ashes, is important not because it's the practice of any particular denomination. Rather, purification, it relates to a much broader appeal to our spiritual health. By realizing our sinful, fallen state and our need for purification, it lifts Easter's magnificence, making it shine all the brighter.

Our repentant hearts and our cleansed consciences help us to better realize the enormity of God's grace that He showed us on the Cross.

How Close Are You?

READINGS: PSALM 27

As we step further into Lent, we are naturally drawn to the need to pray. Much has been written about prayer methods and processes, many offering catchy acronyms to help us structure our prayers so words will perfectly flow. All are good if they inspire a person to actually pray. For many people, these are all helpful and needed tools.

But sometimes we complicate what God wants us to keep simple. St. Teresa of Avila, the 16th century mystic, wrote '*The closer one approaches to God, the simpler one becomes.*'

In the Old Testament, the shortest prayer – just 5 words – was by Moses. He spoke from the immediacy of the fear that weighed on his heart as his sister stood before him, white with leprosy.

Oh God, please heal her. ~Numbers 12.13

In the New Testament, Peter is walking on the water. He begins to sink and cries out a 3-word prayer. Just

like Moses, he spoke only what needed to be said out
of the immediacy of his fear as he started to sink
below the surface of the water.

Lord, save me. ~Matthew 14.30

Both prayers were uttered within mere feet of God.
Saying just what needed to be said.

The closer…the simpler.

Are You Praying or Performing?

READINGS: PSALM 145; MATTHEW 6.5-8

According to Merriam-Webster dictionary, a hypocrite is *a person who puts on a false appearance of virtue or religion.*

In Matthew, Jesus taught us that hypocrites pray to be noticed by others, putting on a *false appearance* of piety and self-righteousness so that people would reward them for their many words and flashy presentation skills.

Jesus said this is not the way to do it. Instead he taught us that we need to be noticed by no one except Him. *Go into your room and shut the door.* Not to perform for Him, but to simply pray. In secret. Alone. With Him. Just as Jesus did.

He would withdraw to desolate places and pray. ~Luke 5.16

God knew full well that it would be hard for us not to judge ourselves when we are in performance mode. *What are others thinking about me? Was I loud*

*enough or profound enough or good enough? Will
they think I am a loser if I say it that way?*

Fortunately, when our prayers cease being a
performance, and become a heartfelt conversation
with our Father - <u>either publicly or privately</u> - praying
gets real simple.

Short, long, transparent, heartfelt, honest, even
silent…whatever it needs to be, we just need to go in,
close the door, and open our hearts in prayer. He's
waiting.

Can Your 'Now' Be Used for Your 'Forever?'

READINGS: PSALM 27; PHILIPPIANS 1.19-30

Thomas asked the question that was probably on the other disciples' minds. "Lord we do not where you are going? How can we know the way?" Jesus replied, "I am the way, the truth and the life." He made it clear: It's him, or it's nothing.

We often don't act like we believe that, living like a wandering tourist rather than as a sojourner on a focused journey towards heaven.

> *For we know that if the tent that is our earthly home is destroyed, we have a building from God, a house not made with hands, eternal in the heavens.*
> ~2 Corinthians 5.1,5

The eternal neighborhood awaits us. It has already been erected. The plumbing works and the lights are on. When we leave this earthly 'tent' it will be with celebration as we join Jesus in the forever home he has already prepared.

On the Way

Come you who are blessed by my
Father, inherit the kingdom prepared
for you from the foundation of the
world. ~Matthew 25.34

But here in our in-between time – in our earthly tent
awaiting our eternal home – we need only to seek
what God has for us here, in the immediate, that can
be used for His eternal glory.

Our *now* being used for His *forever*.

What Lies Before You?

READINGS: PSALM 23; ROMANS 12.1-2

In the fictional *Book Thief*, the narrator of the story (i.e., death) describes the passing away of one person with these words: "Her whole death was now ahead of her." A phrase jam-packed with consequence.

What lies ahead for believers is an eternity with God in that home that was bought and paid for by Jesus' work on the Cross.

For those who do not choose Jesus, death will be altogether different. They didn't choose God *here*, so don't get to be with Him *there*. Yet, death will be the same for both: their *whole death is ahead of them*.

> *I told you that you would die in your sins, for unless you believe that I am he you will die in your sins.* ~John 8.24

So now we move ahead, not as idler wanderers, but as pilgrims on a quest to get home. And along the way, we will change. We will grow. For it is on this path where we experience God, getting comfortable and ever more grateful with the idea of an eternity with the God of the Universe.

It is here, on the way of Jesus, where we learn the will of God for our life in this temporary tent. And it is on this way where we are transformed into the image of our Lord. [see 2 Corinthians 3.18]

Is Your Faith Moving?

READINGS: ISAIAH 40

Our faith is in constant movement. Perhaps we don't sense it in times of stillness but when we grow tired and weary of battling against the world it is like our faith is nowhere to be found. We feel like we are treading water, getting nowhere fast.

Even then our faith is growing. For out of every battle comes new muscle, and out of that new muscle comes the strength to get moving again.

Let's be realistic. When we are deep in the battlefield, it's not so easy to be calm in that assurance. Battling the world's siren call often looks a whole lot more inviting than the view of faith from the middle of the fast-moving river current.

But trust grows in the midst of the waiting for the strength to make it through. Trusting that God will arrive in time before you drown. Trusting that the everlasting God will never forget his promise that He told Isaiah.

They who wait for the Lord shall
renew their strength; they shall run

On the Way

*and not be weary, they shall walk and
not faint. ~Isaiah 40.31*

It's often when hanging by that proverbial thread, that the thread thickens *while* we hang onto it.

He sees all of it, and He never tires of helping us.

How Often Will He Embrace You?

READINGS: LUKE 15.11-32

God knows us so well. He knows when we falter in our faith. He knows when we forget what it meant for His Son to die on the Cross. In this season, that sounds so ugly, doesn't it? But God gets it because He gets us.

He does not faint or grow weary; his
understanding is unsearchable.
~Isaiah 40.28

Unsearchable. Unfathomable. Mysterious. About everything and everybody.

When our forgetful minds and hearts turn away, He understands that for us to return to Him will not be easy. When we do, it is party time!

The story of the Prodigal Son teaches that so well! God knows that when we turn back, as the wandering son did, it has taken a humbling effort to turn our prideful, self-centered hearts back. He so loves that about us, for when we are humbled, we are truly, at least for that moment, all His.

On the Way

I would rather be a doorkeeper in the house of my God than dwell in the tents of wickedness. ~Psalm 84.10

And there is another faith-strengthener that we receive when we turn back. We get to see our Father waiting at the end of the road. Arms opened wide. Smile on His face.

The Cross enables us to run back into His arms every time, over and over again. And over and over He will stretch wide His arms and embrace us once again.

Are You As Bold As Your Forgiveness?

READINGS: MICAH 7.18-20; LUKE 7.36-50

Repentance is a hidden gem of our faith. We don't even see the need for it until we see how dark our sin has become.

It is part of a massive chain reaction in our hearts. First we become painfully aware of our sin. Then, as we feel the weight of that sin, we repent, turning away from the sin, choosing to no longer partake in it. Then forgiveness flows. All three steps need to be there. If one link is missing, the whole thing misfires.

> *If we say we have not sinned, we make him a liar, and his word is not in us. ~1 John 1.10*

In the story in Luke, Jesus' feet are washed in tears, kissed and anointed with expensive oil by a woman of dubious character, described as a 'sinner,' who entered the home of a Pharisee, uninvited. Her repentance was palpable in her display of love.

The Bible doesn't tell us where she would have interacted with Jesus to experience such release.

On the Way

Perhaps she was at the back of the crowd, or among a crowd of thousands who ate from a basket that never emptied. It doesn't matter as much as realizing how much her heart must have been changed to do what she did.

Her sins, which are many, are forgiven – for she loved much. ~Luke 7.47

Learning that Jesus was there, this sinner just walked right into a Pharisee's house, uninvited. There is a boldness in the forgiven.

Tomorrow, we learn that in Simon, the Pharisee, we see a different story.

Do You Have A Missing Link?

READINGS: PSALM 32; 1 JOHN 1.5-10

We pick up the story from yesterday as the woman is wiping Jesus' feet and anointing them from her alabaster jar. What a beautiful scene of love!

The host, Simon the Pharisee, did not even look at this woman. His glance at her as she entered the house told him everything he needed to know. She was a sinner, which by his attitude proclaimed himself to be the opposite.

The 3-step chain reaction of forgiveness was already missing a link, and without that first link – awareness – the 2nd one – repentance – had nowhere to link.

Did he not see her tears, her uninhibited show of joy and gratitude? Did he miss completely that she was so moved that she did the unthinkable by entering his house to begin with?

The light has come into the world,
and people loved the darkness rather
than the light because their works
were evil. ~John 3.19

On the Way

What kind of love, knowing we are often much like Simon, takes all of our punishment on himself?

Simon never got it. We say that we get it, but often fail to show it. Today, let's pause and let that truth knock us off our feet anew, right at his feet to cry ourselves out with gratitude.

Do You Need More Proof?

READINGS: PSALM 77; LUKE 5.12-16

Early in Jesus' ministry, Jesus healed a man with leprosy with just a touch of his hand and a few words. Then he directed the man to do a curious thing. (Which he also did when he healed the 10 lepers in Luke 17.)

He told him to go to the Jewish priest for the ritual cleansing that was decreed in the Law in Leviticus 14 as proof of the healing. This was something that had only been recorded 3 times in all of the Scriptures (Miriam, Namaan, Uzziah).

> *If I do them, even though you do not believe me, believe the works, that you may know and understand that the Father is in me, and I am in the Father. ~John 10.38*

Jesus never wanted to be noticed for **the works of healing** unless it pointed people toward the authority he had from God. His was no magic act to attract followers. His was a ministry that was noticed for its power that could only have come from God. By healing the men of leprosy, he completed what the Law had started. And the priests were forced to verify that.

Their healing provided yet another layer of evidence that he was undeniably the Son of God.

Who Defines Your Worth?

READINGS: PSALM 103; 1 JOHN 2:15-17

Many of us think that our worth is in how useful we are – to our family, to our employer, to our church community. Yes, we should give ourselves in service to all of that, but are we more worthy because we are more *useful* to others? Do we self-identify with the results, selling out to the grade-givers rather than the life-giver?

Jesus was about to be murdered. He could have asked his Father to bring fire down on his accusers. Instead, he totally ignored the haters and spent his last hours praying for his disciples and for all of us who would eventually believe in his name. Isn't it curious that he chose to do that even as he was about to become completely unsuccessful in the eyes of the world?

Henri Nouwen observed that when we don't keep our eyes on Jesus we are apt to feel worthwhile *only* when we have successes as defined by the world.

*See to it that no one takes you
captive by philosophy and empty
deceit, according to human tradition,*

29

On the Way

*according to the elemental spirits of
the world, and not according to
Christ. ~Colossians 2.8*

Jesus did not confuse who or what defined him. As a believer, we need to do that same. The world and all of its allure does not define who we are. God alone does and He always gives us a passing grade.

Are You In the Fog?

READINGS: PSALM 119.25-32

Jesus didn't go to the Cross to give us what the world has already offered – the temporary, empty, fickle stuff that is here today, and gone tomorrow. Instead, he came to give us something beyond what anyone or anything in the world can ever give.

> *The world is passing away along with its desires, but whoever does the will of God abides forever. ~1 John 2.17*

To be 'in the world but not of the world' takes a realistic awareness of God's view of the world. To be 'of the world' wreaks of the temporal idea of living for today. We may look right but in reality may be living a spiritual masquerade with some Christian-speak slathered all over world values.

Every time we grab hold of something of this world to make us feel worthwhile, it's like trying to grab a handful of fog that quickly disappears between our fingers.

On the Way

*But you are a chosen race, a royal
priesthood, a holy nation, a people for
his own possession, that you may
proclaim the excellencies of him who
called you out of darkness into his
marvelous light. ~1 Peter 2.9*

Our worth is completely secure in this: God has called
us out of the world's darkness into His marvelous
light. Jesus died so we could live outside of the
blurriness of the world's fog. In finding that clarity, we
have found our worth in the arms of God.

Is Your Life on Stable Ground?

READINGS: PSALM 102; MATTHEW 7.24-27

Our culture moves at breakneck speed. Just look at the rapidly expanding, insanely fast-launching updates to any computer you own. Add to that the 24/7 news cycle that blasts at us from a hundred directions, insisting on notice and reaction, begging by its droning and repetition to carry it with us like a weight across our shoulders.

Each minute, we have a choice to trust in the constancy of change, grasping at each new bauble and sound byte the world offers. Or we can choose to hang onto our God who is completely, consistently stable. He never changes. He never doesn't exist. We can count on that every day. Now and forever.

> *"I am the Alpha and the Omega,"*
> *says the Lord God, "who is and who*
> *was and who is to come, the*
> *Almighty." ~Revelation 1.8*
>
> *Jesus Christ is the same yesterday*
> *and today and forever. ~Hebrews*
> *13.8*

On the Way

The grass withers, the flower fades,
but the word of our God will stand
forever. ~Isaiah 40.8

There is great strength in that level of stability but it means nothing if we don't live each day reflecting that foundation. Choosing God first and foremost, anchors our life to His firm foundation.

Is God Your Trendsetter?

READINGS: PSALM 1; 2 CORINTHIANS 5.14-21

As trends shift, as the new becomes old, as styles and colors and even food changes in popularity, it can become quite dizzying to keep up. Even 'vintage' style can be cool today, and out of date *again* tomorrow.

But with God, there are no trends. We don't need to figure out what's new or noteworthy, whether we are trending with the latest fad, or up to date on any 'cool jargon.' We need not search for anything beyond His word to verify how God transcends any trend this world has to offer.

God says we are new creations. ~2 Corinthians 5.17

God says we are loved, unceasingly. ~Lamentations 3.22-23

God says we are chosen. ~1 Thessalonians 1.4

God says we are free from our sin. ~John 8.36

On the Way

There is nothing out of fashion, out of date, or vintage about our life in Christ. It never needs an update, never trends itself out of fashion, never delivers hopelessness. The love that took Christ from a Cross to an empty tomb endures. It is truly new every morning. Forever.

Are You Patient in the Ripening?

READINGS: PSALM 27; LUKE 8.4-15

The parable of the sower and soils has been studied and scrutinized for a couple of thousand years. Although it most often related to salvation, it also is an apt description of our hearts as they ebb and flow through our life of faith.

> *As for that in the good soil, they are those who, hearing the word, hold it fast in an honest and good heart, and bear fruit with patience. ~Luke 8.15*

This verse highlights three attributes that define those who have good soil:

- **Hearing the word** is about reading and letting our mind absorb the teaching, listening to sermons, discussing with one another the wonder of it.
- **Holding fast to it** means to take it everywhere you go, never letting go of it. That could be a memorized verse, or a small Bible that you refer to, even and app on your phone.

- **Bearing fruit with patience**. This may be the hardest one of all for we must wait for God's timing to work out the fruit production.

It is the latter of these three that may take the most prayer. But a good heart is worth pursuing, as if searching for a long lost treasure.

Is Your Soil Producing?

READINGS: MATTHEW 13.18-23

The parable of the soils is so much like a life of faith. Sometimes it produces great fruit, and sometimes the just gets depleted.

We get weary. We forget to do our daily Bible reading. We don't pray our way through a day, or two, or three. We don't memorize any scripture or review even the few we may know. We let our faith slip into bad soil conditions. When our soil gets depleted we tend to forget God's faithfulness and goodness.

To bounce back quickly from this slippage, we need to be aware that trials aren't just in-your-face temptations and afflictions. Trials are also of the heart, invisible to others, but all too crystal clear to God. An untended heart, just like all of our trials and afflictions, will, when faced and conquered, produce steadfastness.

Count it all joy, when you meet trials of various kind, for you know that the testing of your faith produces steadfastness. ~James 1.2-3

On the Way

Our life of faith, just like the soil in a garden, isn't a once and done event. It will not naturally stay fertile. We need to be soil tenders, making sure we give it all it needs to stay healthy, ready to produce fruit.

Let us not grow weary of doing good,
for in due season we will reap, if we
do not give up. ~Galatians 6.9

Will You Get Scorched On Your Way In?

READINGS: PSALM 42; 1 CORINTHIANS 3.10-15

There is much responsibility involved in a life totally sold out to God. It carries great accountability with it, reflecting the power that is inherent in it.

Many take it lightly, considering Jesus' sacrifice their fire insurance against the fires of hell, a sort of get-out-of-jail-free card. It was certainly never free for Jesus, was it? He paid an incredibly heavy price for what so many accept so casually and then park on a shelf in their garage.

Grace certainly allows for that choice of truncated faith, but there will still be a reckoning for what we did with this great gift.

For we must all appear before the judgement seat of Christ, so that each one may receive what is due for what he has done in the body, whether good or evil. ~2 Corinthians 5.10

Paul taught that a life lived this way will be like one barely escaping a fire, its flames literally lapping at your heels. You'll get to heaven but will you have a life that was honoring to God? Will you be able to say to God – face-to-face – that you maximized the gifts he had given you for His glory?

What a loss for those who choose this kind of faith, rather than the life that God had intended when they chose Him.

Are You OK With Where God Has You Now?

READINGS: GENESIS 16.7-15; 1 CORINTHIANS 7.17-24

Jesus was a man of his time, yet his universal approach to life fit everywhere, both in Old and New Testament time, and even today.

When Hagar treated her mistress badly, she was the one in error. Yet God saw her heart as she fled into the wild. He noticed her, this slave from Egypt. She was hurt, afraid and pregnant. She knew she had nowhere to go since Sarai had kicked her out. But God knew that this slave needed to know that the God of Israel was there for her too.

> *There is neither Jew nor Greek, there is neither slave nor free, there is no male or female, for you are all one in Christ Jesus. ~Galatians 3.8*

God has always seen us. Each one of us. Where we were, and where we are.

On the Way

Even the slaves of the New Testament times would wonder if the salvation Jesus talked of was for them as well. Jesus did not let them down, assuring them of the exact same Gospel as everyone else.

He didn't release anyone from the role they were playing. Rather, he showed them a better way to live, broader than just the immediate, right where they were. He was showing them eternity.

What Are Your Chains?

READINGS: ISAIAH 9.1-7; HEBREWS 2.14-18

It's not hard to empathize with Hagar at the moment she sat in the wild all by herself. Filled with fear and hopelessness, she was not only a slave in Sarai's household, she was also a slave to the emptiness in her own heart. She saw her whole existence through the invisible chains that held her so tightly, both physically and spiritually.

Just as God saw Hagar's situation, and her heart, Jesus sees us. He sees the chains we allow to tighten around ourselves, and the frame of slavery through which we see our life. He went to the Cross to change that.

> *I will go before you and will level the mountains; I will break down gates of bronze and cut through bars of iron.*
> *~Isaiah 45.2*

His plan was never about changing things into what we humans want. His plan was so much bigger than our shortsighted conditions. It was about showing us, through a real life, living example, a better way.

45

On the Way

There is nothing that enslaves our heart that God cannot break through. It is the message of the Empty Tomb. He defeated death, so He can defeat any fear that grips us, any worry that wakes us at night, any loneliness that seeps into our mind.

There is nothing that can take a hold on us that He has not already defeated.

Are You Going It Alone?

READINGS: DEUTERONOMY 30.15-20; HEBREWS 4.15-16

Ours is not an easy faith. It often feels like an uphill battle between the world and the freedom that God has offered us at the Cross.

We say 'yes' to our salvation in Jesus, then turn around and scream 'no' to the freedom of the empty tomb. Our hearts grow lukewarm, even cold, to things of the faith. We say 'no' when we take even baby steps towards the ugliness of worldly scintillations.

The Bible teaches us to walk away from love of worldly-everything, deny our own worldly-driven desires and take up our own cross. This all too often brings us into puddles of frustration that are hard to get through.

That's the reality of the Gospel. So simple, yet so hard. We get strengthened in Bible study only to see the clarity and simplicity leak out of us in the heat of the world. It is the catch that entangles us as we try to do it with just our measly human abilities.

On the Way

*Trust in the Lord with all your heart
and do not lean on your own
understanding. In all your ways
acknowledge Him and He will make
straight your paths. ~Proverbs 3.5-6*

God knew it would be like this, that we would struggle
if we tried to do it alone. He had watched the
Israelites try it that way for centuries. We needed not
only a way out, but a way to get through.

Easter gave us a forever home. But it also gave us
the strength for the journey that will get us there.

Are You Blindly Groping Around?

READINGS: PSALM 107; EPHESIANS 2.11-22

There are inevitable times in a life of faith that we will seem dark. Sometimes it will be because of our wrong thinking, our own wrong turns taking us far away from God. Other times it may just be a time of silence that God brings us to for whatever divine reason.

However we got there, there is always a way out. The truth remains. If we calm our minds long enough and listen closely enough to what we already know about our God, He will never let us down.

> *They should seek God, and perhaps feel their way toward him and find him. Yet he is actually not far from each one of us. ~Acts 17.27 {ESV}*

What a reality-smacking verse!

We *feel our way toward him*, crawling along on all fours, blindly groping for a glimmer of light, for a rock to grasp in the rising waters.

On the Way

Isn't it comforting to read those words: *He is actually not far from each one of us?* He's close not just to those whose faith appears to be so bright and carefree compared to your current state of darkness. He is right next to *each one of us*. All the time.

We just need to *feel our way toward Him*, to find him right there, next to us.

What Love Is This?

READINGS: ISAIAH 55; PHILIPPIANS 1.8-11

Ken Boa, pastor and author, wrote "Love as the world defines is anemic; it's a thin broth, unable to sustain a robust relationship. We need something more."

> *So Jacob served seven years for Rachel, and they seemed to him but a few days because of the love he had for her. ~Genesis 29.20*

What a romantic verse. And Jacob actually ended up working another 7 years for the love of his life. True Harlequin romance potential! Yet even that kind of love is still anemic compared to what God offers us.

What then defines a non-anemic kind of love? What does the God-kind of love look like, the kind we stand in awe of at the Cross?

Undeserved – loving like God is loving those who don't deserve it.

Unassuming – assuming there will be no reciprocation of the same.

Undeniable – doing it for no other reason than love.

Unprovoked – we didn't ask for it; we didn't even know we needed it.

Unrelenting – it never, ever stops; it never changes; no matter what we do.

See what kind of love the Father has given us that we should be called children of God; and so we are. ~1 John 3.1

Are You A Part of the Circle?

READINGS: 1ST CORINTHIANS 13

The love of God, His agape love, is truly incredible. When we actually grasp at least a portion, it is not hard to understand how impossible it would be for humans to conjure this up on our own.

Greater love has no one than this, that someone lay down his life for his friends. ~John 15.13

Jesus said that a true friend would die for his friend, if his love was as great as the love God showed us on the Cross. But let's be honest. How many of us would actually see that as an option? Even at our best, we are hard-pressed to imagine doing that, let alone stretching out our arms for strangers. But Jesus did.

In this, the love of God was made manifest among us, that God sent his only Son into the world, so that we might live through him. If we love one another, God abides in us and his love is perfected In us. ~1 John 4.9,12

We cannot love like God. But we can have the love of God abiding in us and show it to others. His love is made operational through us by the work of Jesus on the Cross.

It is a great big circle of love!

Is Your Heart Aligned?

READINGS: ISAIAH 58

In Isaiah 58, God issues a powerful warning about fasting. We cannot fast with the wrong attitude and expect any answers from God. It's not unlike many of the warnings in the Bible that address our heart issues. It is serious business to have our heart right before we attempt anything!

But there are 2 verses, just past those on fasting, that are worth pausing on.

> *If you take away the yoke from your midst, the pointing of the finger and speaking wickedness, if you pour yourself out for the hungry and satisfy the desire of the afflicted, **then** shall your light rise in the darkness and your gloom be as the noonday.*
> *~Isaiah 58.9-10*

After reading those sobering thoughts, we must ask ourselves these questions:

- Have I put yokes of judgment on those around me that have made them feel guilty, or ashamed?
- Do I point an accusing, pride-filled finger at anyone?
- Do I speak with a tongue that drips of wickedness?
- Have I given anything to help the poor and afflicted?

For where your treasure is, there your heart will be also. ~Matthew 6.21

Out of the abundance of the heart, the mouth speaks. ~Luke 6.45

Do You Forget to Thank?

READINGS: PSALM 106

A self-centered life is a self-applauded one, for sure. But it can be an ungrateful one, as well.

In Luke, we learn that Jesus healed 10 men who were suffering with leprosy. These men had been forced to live apart from their town and family for years. If a leper even walked close to another person he had to shout out 'unclean, unclean' so that others could steer away. It was a lonely, demeaning way to live.

The story goes that of the 10 men that he healed, only one returned to thank him.

Maybe it was the long-term pain and shame of the disease that clouded their sense of politeness. Or they were overwhelmed at their smooth and scabless skill that they forgot that gratitude was in order. No matter the reason behind it, their eyes were centered on themselves. It is a scenario we can easily understand, and perhaps even mirror in different ways in our own lives.

On the Way

One of the men did return to thank Jesus for healing him. He was a Samaritan who, by virtue of being a Samaritan, would have known what being ostracized from a community felt like long before the first blemish of disease showed up.

Perhaps his healing was about more than just clean skin. Perhaps his gratitude was more about receiving the freedom of Christ.

If the Son sets you free, you will be free indeed. ~John 8.36

Are You Trusting God to Provide?

READINGS: PSALM 23

The wilderness and the garden. The two places Jesus struggled in his human existence. In the wilderness, he was tempted to do something other than what he was there to do. In the garden, he questioned if there were a better way to accomplish his purpose in being there.

In both situations, he struggled with much the same physical challenges as we do. In the first, he was hungry, and physically weakened. In the second, he was anxious, and seeking a different way out.

Both times he was alone. Both times were turning points in his ministry on earth – one to kick it off, and one to bring it to a close. Both times God brought ministering angels to his side.

After not eating for 40 days, and after battling with Satan, God provided comfort.

On the Way

Then the devil left him, and behold,
angels came and were ministering to
him. ~Matthew 4.11

Anguishing over what was to come, asking for a different way, not turning away from the inevitable, God provided strength.

There appeared to him an angel,
strengthening him. ~Luke 22.43

God provides for us as well: just what we need, just when we need it.

What Do Your Actions Show God?

READINGS: GENESIS 22

Abraham was about to kill his only son. In complete trust in God, he obeyed God. God did not tell him the reason, or the outcome, or any of the details about this one situation.

But He told Abraham to trust him, to remember his words, to believe that what He said He was going to do, He would do. Abraham chose to believe it all, and to act on that belief.

We all know the end of the story. At the moment before he slit his son's throat, God provided a ram for the sacrifice. God kept His promise.

Abraham called that place Jehovah Jireh: the Lord will Provide.

> *Now I know that you fear God seeing*
> *you have not withheld your son, your*
> *only son, from me. ~Genesis 22.12*

"Now I know." With each of our actions of obedience, with each time we choose faith in God rather than the things of our temporary world, God knows that we love Him.

If you love me, you will keep my commandments. ~John 14.15

How Wide Is Your Worship?

READINGS: PSALM 19

God created the heavens and the earth. That means He created the earth's atmosphere to be exactly as it is, with blue beams of light from the sun He created, hitting our atmosphere at just the right angle, disbursing across the air particles to give us the blueness of our skies.

And then He went a step further. In each of us, He created our eyes with little cells called cones and rods that help us see this reflected light – in fact, there are 6 million cones and 110 million rods in each of our eyes just to process the colors of our world, including the blue of the sky!

But He wasn't finished yet. One last detail. He gave us all a heart that loves the color of the sky. What if we all hated sky blue? A sunny day would be downright depressing, right? Without this step the whole thing falls apart.

But God never leaves out any detail. Not one.

On the Way

Let the field exult, and everything in it!
Than shall all the trees of the forest
sing for joy. ~Psalm 96.12

Knowing that attention to detail to just one color of a whole rainbow, we cannot confine our 'worship' to a narrow window of a Sunday morning. We need a much broader stance to take in all of that majesty of God's creation and how very worthy He is to be worshipped.

Do You Take the Time to Hear?

READINGS: 1 SAMUEL 3; JOHN 14.25-30

One of the most beautiful scenes of Easter happens at the empty tomb with Mary Magdalene. Luke tells us in his gospel that Jesus had driven evil spirits out of her, and that she was one of several women who traveled with Jesus and his disciples through cities and villages proclaiming and bringing the good news of the kingdom of God (Luke 8.1-2).

She finds the tomb empty and speaks with a man she assumed to be the gardener. Turning away from him, the man whispers her name. She recognizes that voice. She has heard it many times. She had been so close to it, so inspired by it, so loved by it.

> *He goes before them, and the sheep*
> *follow him, for they know his voice.*
> *~John 10.4*

We cannot expect to hear the voice of God, to know what His will is for our life, to be comforted by His promises, if we do not take the time to be close to him. To listen for His voice through His word; through prayer; through worship

Oh that our every interaction with God would be one in which we hear clear words, that every Bible study we would see verses almost popping off the page, the exact ones to meet our need at that exact moment. But it doesn't happen that way. At least not always. But given time, we will recognize what God is saying. With time, we will know His voice intimately and clearly.

Let's give it some time.

What's Blocking Your View?

READINGS: EXODUS 20.1-17; MATTHEW 19.16-30

One of the better-known conversations that Jesus had during his ministry was with the rich young man.

Jesus began by giving the young man some confidence by asking him if he followed a few of the commandments. Jesus did not list all of them. In fact, he left out half of them, including the first one: *You shall have no other God before me.*

By this time the young man must have been leaning in, eager to hear what would get him the golden ticket.

Jesus made it clear that the one thing the man needed to do was to get rid of all his earthly possessions. Not just some of them. Not a hefty percentage of them. All of them. If he did, there would be a reward, and then he could come follow him. He gave him a clear directive, a clear reward, and a clear next step. We know how the story ends.

> *The idols of the nations are silver and gold, the work of human hands. Those who make them become like*

On the Way

them, so do all who trust in them.
~Psalm 135.15,18

Anything that stops our choosing God can be an idol. Even when truth punches us in the face, we cannot see past the idol that sits in between. Our idol is a treasure we think will last. But it's blocking the view of the only One that does.

Does Your Idol Look Different?

READINGS: EXODUS 32.1-6

There is nothing we can do that God won't love us through. But He knows in his infinite and unwavering wisdom, that when we follow His direction, we will gain so much more than the world could ever give.

But the world's stuff is right in front of us, visually alluring. Our God-given senses are alive with the smells and sounds of it. We even find some security when we grasp it our fingers.

The Israelites waited just a month for Moses to return from talking with God before they intentionally turned away to another god. They constructed an idol to worship, made from the very gold jewelry that the Egyptians had given them when they left captivity. They were worshipping and celebrating a golden calf made from their plunder!

We can scoff at such self-centered foolishness, but none of our present-day idolatry looks any different to God. None of It Is new to Him. He has seen it all since He created Adam and Eve.

On the Way

*Jesus, looking at him, loved him, and
said to him, 'You lack one thing…
~Mark 10.20 {ESV}*

The love of the Cross still ignores our petty idolatry,
our selfishness, our foolish disregard for the things of
God. He loves us anyway. But what could an idol-free
life with Him look like?

Are We All In?

READINGS: DEUTERONOMY 11; 1ST JOHN 2.15-19

There are so many stories in the Bible that are timeless in their relevance. The rich young man is one of those stories. His blind desire to embrace both worlds reflects our world today as if in a mirror: Have what we have here and get what we want there.

We don't walk away from God because we don't get an answer. We walk away because we refuse to do it His way. We want to get 'there' – life with Him – without leaving 'here' – our worldly life and all its stuff.

What God wants us to do seems so uncomfortable, so unpopular. Like the young man, we want to hear we can have it all without any change. We want desperately to hold tight to what we have, not realizing that if we don't let go we cannot grasp what is better.

So we fix our eyes not on what is seen but on what is unseen. For what is seen is temporal, but what is not seen is eternal. ~2 Corinthians 4.18

God wanted the young man, and us, to choose to be all-in with His Son, so we can have all that is worth having. Not just a little of his blessings, but all of them.

Jesus loved us through the work on the Cross to make that possible.

Could We Be So Focused?

READINGS: MATTHEW 21.1-17

There was cheering and singing when Jesus rode into town that Sunday. The people were so excited to welcome Jesus to the city. They spread their cloaks and branches from trees in front of him. As he rode on a small donkey, it would have been hard to distinguish him from those walking upright around him.

Yet the people found him. The people always found him.

> They shouted 'Hosanna, to the Son of David. Blessed is he who comes in the name of the Lord! Hosanna in the highest!' ~Matthew 21.9

It was certainly not the same kind of parade that the Romans had when they came to town. The most important of them would ride on the largest horses so they could be seen by all. Their steads would have been decorated with gold and plumes of peacocks. It would not be a mystery to the people who they should fake a waver or two towards.

On the Way

Jesus could care less if he was noticed, as long as they noticed his Father. So, he continued his work as if his own murder was not imminent.

He cleared the temple of those who did not belong which made room for those who needed his help. He healed many who were blind and lame, as children danced and sang. He just went about his Father's business.

Five days later he did what he came to do.

We are going up to Jerusalem…to be crucified…and will be raised on the third day. ~Matthew 20.17-19

Are You Afraid to Ask?

READINGS: PSALM 119.33-40; JAMES 1.1-8

The Bible records a smattering of what Jesus did in his 3-year ministry here on earth. John tells us that if everything were recorded that Jesus did the world could not contain the books that would be written. {John 21.25)

The disciples were front and center for all of it. And like us as we read the word today, they probably could not remember or even understand all of it, even though they were eye witnesses to it.

> *They did not understand the saying and were afraid to ask him. ~Mark 9.32*

Today we have all of Jesus' teachings in one book. We can study it back and forth, and in different order, and by 4 different Gospel perspectives. For them, it was the Old Testament, the rabbis and Jesus. And some of what Jesus taught was downright confusing. And scary.

On the Way

We know the end of the story. They did not. Their fear and uncomfortableness with some of Jesus' teaching was not surprising.

But today, we need not be afraid of asking. Without shame or embarrassment. Through His Spirit, He already knows that we do not know.

And He already loves that we depend on Him for understanding.

Is the Word Alive or Dead?

READINGS: PSALM 1; 2ND TIMOTHY 3.15-17

Probiotics are beneficial bacteria that live in our intestine. Supplementing our diet with these good bacteria, helps maintain our health, strengthening any weak areas of our digestive health.

Probiotics are living organisms that we put in our body.

Similar in so many ways to what we do with the word of God.

> *The word of God is living and active, sharper than any two-edged sword, piercing to the division of soul and spirit, of joints and of marrow, and discerning the thoughts and intentions of the heart. ~Hebrews 4.12*

It is living, active, sharp, piercing, and discerning. The word of God is not just a bunch of words, a cool story, an impressive book of knowledge. Ingesting it into our hearts, is not just an exercise in good Christian living.

On the Way

It has a purpose. It does not just lay around doing nothing. It does so much more.

It takes us where we are, and shapes us, carves us, and makes us aware of exactly where our heart stands in relation to God's truths. But just as with a probiotic supplement, we cannot let it lay on the counter and just look it. We have to absorb it into our heart.

It works inside of us even when we don't feel it or believe it. You put it in, it will do its work.

It is spiritual probiotics; except better.

What Value Are the Unnoticed?

READINGS: EXODUS 1.15-21; HEBREWS 6.9-12

We all know who Jesus' earthly father was. But we know little of Joseph's life once Jesus is safely housed in Nazareth. He was around long enough to father a few more children with Mary, but other than that, we don't know what happened to him.

Yet his impact on the ministry of Jesus cannot ever be overstated. Christmas had to happen exactly as it did, and it could not have done so without Joseph's willingness to obey completely. It was vital in the whole trajectory of God's plan for Easter.

Like Joseph, we may sometimes feel that our existence will fade into obscurity having little impact or influence to affect anything for God. Yet, faith is often most powerful in obscurity, for it's there that we rely on God alone. We are not distracted with applause or tweets or snapchats or text messages.

It is better to take refuge in the Lord
than to trust in man. ~Psalm 118.8

On the Way

God uses a different set of measurements than the world does. His include things like faithfulness, obedience, trust. He doesn't give a rip if the world ever notices that we have taught 100 Bible studies, or spoken in front of audiences of thousands, or written a bazillion notes of encouragement. All are good things but not if they are done with a heart that is not seeking after God.

To gain his notice, his applause, takes counter culture obedience.

On the Way

Who Do You Love?

READINGS: LUKE 22.15-16

It was Thursday, the day before all of history would change. These 12 men had been with him for 3 years. They witnessed the reality of the Son of God unfold before them with each teaching, each healing, each truth spoken to those who thought truth was in their own made-up regulations.

It was friendship's finest feast. He called them friends knowing full well that they would all be overcome with fear and confusion before the sun came up the next day. He loved these men in spite of their ignorance, their slowness to grasp, their impulsiveness.

> *Earth-worms are miserable company*
> *for angels, moles but unhappy*
> *company for eagles, yet love made*
> *our great Master endure the society*
> *of his ignorant and carnal followers.*
> *~Charles Spurgeon, from a sermon*
> *delivered on 5/10/1868*

But he knew he would be going to his destiny soon, leaving them alone. Even so, he was glad to be

81

sharing the last Passover with them, as he prepared to fulfill its prophecy.

He was moved to serve them by washing their feet, by teaching them what we know today as Communion.

You do not realize what I am doing, but later you will understand. ~John 13.7

Do You Have a Good Friday Faith?

READINGS: ISAIAH 43

In the beginning, God came to earth and created a creature in His image who would have free choice to love Him. He put them in a beautiful garden so He could walk with them through its beauty. I can imagine that He taught them both to whistle as they strolled through the beauty of His creation with His creation.

Then sin entered. And things changed. This creation could no longer hang out in the Garden and whistle their days away. Now they had to be banished.

On Christmas, God again left heaven, and came down here to His creation to bring them back to His side. Even as the baby Jesus grew, Good Friday loomed on the horizon. It had always been the plan.

> *For I have come down from heaven,*
> *not to do my own will but the will of*
> *him who sent me that everyone who*
> *looks on the Son and believes in him*
> *should have eternal life. ~John 6. 38,*
> *40*

Jesus obediently died for the benefit of His Father's creation, for us. Not because of anything he did, but for all that we created beings have done, are doing, and will ever do.

Some believers only get as far as the Cross in their faith. They accept the forgiveness that was offered that day. And that's certainly a wondrous thing.

But they never walk to the Tomb to find the freedom of its emptiness. There is more to Easter than just the Cross for we get to whistle with God once again.

Can You Hold On Until Tomorrow?

READINGS: PSALM 130; ROMANS 5.1-11

Saturday. The day after Jesus was so brutally murdered. It is a Sabbath day for the Jews, a day of rest. It seemed even the dead body of Jesus rested on this day. The drama and excitement had quieted after the adrenaline-rush of watching 3 men die, the weird darkening of the sun, the Temple curtain vandalized.

For the believers, those who had followed and loved him, Jesus was gone. The grief of a mother, of brothers, of friends was overwhelming. His words about coming back were now distant and nebulous. Rest may not come as easy.

> *Come to me, all who labor and are*
> *heavy laden, and I will give you rest.*
> *~Matthew 11.28*

Their minds circling with questions and confusion. The healings. The demons cast out. The resurrection of Lazarus. Walking on water. Calming seas.

On the Way

Their hearts had been changed, they were sure of that. Jesus had not been a charlatan, a fluke. He was the Christ. He was their Messiah.

The sun would rise tomorrow on a day still thick with grief. But there would be hope.

Because they didn't know it yet, but Easter was coming and all will be OK.

This is eternal life, that they know you,

the only true God, and Jesus Christ,

whom you have sent.

I glorified you on earth,

having accomplished the work that

you gave me to do.

~John 17.3-4

It is finished.

~John 19.30

On the Way